THE FATE

OF

CORRUPTI

ON

Dedications

To My Gran, Grandpa,
Mum and Dad For
Believing in me.

JO.FO

To My Freinds amd closest people around me.

JA.FO

Chapter 1

Fourty-nine days until the general election and David Stone a Democratic Party of the United Kingdom MP also known as (DPOTUK) and was running to be the

Prime Minister of the Unkited Kingdom,

It was time for David to go head to head on a television debate against the Leaders of the Liberal Democrats, Conservative Party, Labour Party And UKIP, When David was about to go up to his dressing room he had an urgent telephone call from his wife Mellisa, she told David that she had received a death threat stating "Its me hello again thought you'd never see me again put me up for adoption well im back and im here to get revenge on your new pathetic little family and and one thing start ordering your coffins perry and phillips are the cheapest Bye Pete J Stone Or Marco"

" Mellisa ok I will atempt to try and sneak past the boss it wont be easy but i will try, just promise me you wont go and try anything stupid for Melinda Graces sake please".

" I promise but please hurry David im scared

and im worried that he is going to come in, and put me your dearest wife and Melinda your sweetest baby girl, in excrutiating pain

D D D David you there."

" Mellisa im here and did you say your son so finaly after 20 long lonely years away ignoring us , he returns he was a discrace and a self centred idiotic freak plus he treated you like you you were invisble, and like dirt I am not letting him treat Melinda like that because she is my daughter, and I get a say maybe not with Marco but I do with Melinda okay Mellisa thats final, final I tell you final."

Chapter 2

" David i can hear some one breaking in and i think it might be the idiot we now call Marco"

" Mellisa there is something i need to tell you about Marco"

" No let me tell you something David, there is nothing you know about my son that i dont"

" Well acctualy Mellisa
there is, before he got
adopted I took him to a
Italian restraunt, and
the waiter tripped and 3
pungent slices of Garlic
fell on him and he
screamed in pain and ran
out into the day light and
he was burning and
dragged himself and me
into a dark alley, and
thats when he told me he

was a vampire and the person he was going to live with is his father and his father cant die because he is Count Dracula"

" Mellisa"

" Melinda"

" Oh no I should have told you earlier now he has killed you "

" I am fine an Melinda is to i didnt manage to get any garlic out the cupboard but he is in the house, I am here outside the house"

then David came bursting throught the door, and in the blink of an eye Marco was behind him sinking his sharp,bright white,long fangs into Davids pale thick neck, in anger Mellisa shouted " how dare you turn my husband into a blood sucking monster i had to give you away your father said you will be a dangerous and powerfull V... and didnt even finish and i guess he was trying to say vampire please it is me you want you don't want to kill the little girl oh i wont kill Melinda dad

will he is a vampire now
corrupted by evil then
marco sped up to Mellisa,
and said how dare you
give me up for adoption
and keep her, and then
snapped Mellisa's neck in
half there was thick
blochy blood everywhere
Malleisa's eyes in shock,
Melinda screamed in fear
and through a clove of
garlic at him and ran off

to the local adoption home.

Chapter 3

She was adopted into a nice wealthy family and she went to an Vampire Slaying Academy were she learnt the tips and tricks into being a fearless, ruthless, monster of a vampire slayer, and one day she decided to go back to the dark, desolete, creepy towns of Cardif, after being away for 20 years as she was driving down the streets he got to the beggining of the town as he got out the car dragged her out and said, I am not going into that vampire town so i walked throught and after ten minutes of being in the creepy, dark spinshivering place of a town she realised it was infested with vampires she turned round to see her sick evil father he was so evil that you could se it in his eyes then he saw Marco she pulled a stake out and drove it throught is heart as she watched his eyes glow redder than blood and skin turns blacker than a dark knights sky and then he disintergrated in to dust like a rough cremated being she ran to the nearest cab and drove back home grabbed her car keys and drove to the slaying academy and rounded up the greatest slayers she can find, she opened the big,brown,oak doors and took out the best of the best slaying equipment wich was centurys years old until she was stopped in her tracks ...

<u>Chapter 4</u>

The big,shiny glass door opened, and Proffesor Goodman steped out, she said " you are not going back to Cardiff to slay those vampires until you are fully trained and if you do, we will be the ones there to slay you because you will be the one with the punctured neck.

Melinda agreed and walked to the training room to train for more years to come. She had to eat healthy, and train hard and she had to go vegan so she could eat more vegetables. So after 10 years she was finaly ready she got the greatest slayers and the best equipment and they set off when she got there the vampires where waiting they starting fighting dust scatterd, scortch marks everywhere,rotten lifeless corpses five of

the vampires made a star
and starting chanting the
world starting go black
and shrinking over its
self the slayers killed
the vampires there was
one left and he wiped out
the rest of the
slayersthe vampire tried
to speed of and the
slayer clung on to him
they landed on Jupiter
and they watched as the

Earth grew darker and darker and smaller and smaller until it was nothing for the first couple of days they were trying to kill each other until one day they realised nothing was changing and they had to work together to bring back Earth for both of their kinds and hopefully they could live together

in harmony without
killing each other.

Chapter 5

So they Introduced
themselfs to each other
the vampire said " hello
my name is Apollo son
and heir of Rodriguez
the Great, whats yours"

"My name is Melinda
Grace step daughter of

Count Dracula my brother turned my Father into a blood thirsty evil freak of a man and snapped my mothers neck". (Melinda starts crying heavily and in anger)

The vampire cheers her up and says " I know what happened to your family was horrible but we realy need to get started on saving the Earth".

Melinda mumbled in grief "ok".

Chapter 6

they tried everything like fire balls,spells,super speeding and much more until one day Apollo thought of a great idea of reversing time to the

day of the battle and
stop it from happening,
so he thought of the
spell and repeated it
over and over again in his
head, until he was ready
then he started
chanting, "unos petros
minos time "

the portal opened and
the pair of them stepped
inside, when they
stepped out they

realised that there was a big problem, they went too far back in time for there liking and was in the dinosaur ages Melinda screamed and ran off to hide behind a tree " send us back now " she cried.

"Ok " he replied " unos petros minos time "

Melinda said please be second time lucky as she stepped inside the portal.

This time when stepped out they were standing in the middle of one of the World's most dangerous places "NO MANS LAND" Screamed Melinda and Apollo simultaeneously every second ducking a bullets,

and dodging
Messerschmits and
Hawker Harriot planes.

Chapter 7

They didn't know what
to do every where they
looked they see a dead
soldier with his guts
ripped out and then the
Germans kidnapped them
and took them to them
there head quarters and

tied them up, when they woke up they were opposite a dead English soldiers skeleton Apollo and Melinda was tied up Apollo used his foot to attempt to get a pen knife out of the pocket of the soldier, he cut through the rope and untied Melinda and the super speeded off to a bush to hide so the

Third Reich (Germans)
dont spot them again,
and then he chanted the
spell again " unos petros
minos time "

"OH FOR GOD SAKE
CANT YOU GET ONE
LOUSY SPELL RIGHT
WERE IN ANCIENT
EGYPT!" yelled Melinda
in rage.

" Sorry, I have never said the spell before and i have not practiced it before too"

" EEEWWWW " screached Melinda as she saw Annubis take out Tutankhamun's brains out his nose and stored it in a jar, it was realy goey and stringy and there was a river of dark, red blood oozing out of the Phaoroh's corpse.

" Ouch! " screamed Apollo " this golden, brown sand is to hot don't forget I am a vampire meanwhile smoke was coming of his skin, i think its time to go now "

" I thinks so too " replied Melinda

" unos petros minos time "

" Please be fourth time lucky ".

" Yes yes yes we made it, the battle of vampires vs slayers " cheered Melinda " now we need to stop them from slaughtering each other " as Melinda stepped forwards she cleared her throught " STOOOOP,we are from the future this battle ends badly all slayers and vampires die accept me and Apollo and we had to work together to bring back the Earth and I made a realy good friend on the way, Apollo and he has been so kind and i see no reason why we can't live together in peace and harmony, and we have been through hell to get here we have been to the dinosaur ages, world war 11 the ancient egyption times and now we are here " and then one vampire inturupted " do you know you have been time traveling with a vampire you have brought back Marco with you and your mother "

" OH NO " replied Melinda he is gonna try and kill us "

" watch out " shouted a vampire as he threw a steak and drove it through Marco's heart " OMG " said one of the slayers, " maybe we can trust vampires, after all they just saved Melindas life when Melinda saw her mother in the corner

of her eye, in tears
Melinda ran to her
mother and gave her a
bear hug in happiness
her mother said " Well
done Melinda you did it
Marco is gone and you
have made vampires and
slayers friends "

" mom do you wanna meet
my friend Apollo he is a
vampire "

when Melinda turned around she saw Apollo on one and he said " Melinda I love you so much these few weeks i have spent with you has been the best weeks of my life, so Melinda Grace Stone will you marry me? "

" yes yes of course, I love you too "

6 MONTHS LATER

Apollo and Melinda are married and excpecting a child named Stephan, he will be half vampire half human, he will be the most powerfull baby ever born, and both Melinda and Apollo are expecting the little trouble anytime soon, after weeks of anticipation the baby or you could call it a hybrid came out and left Mellinda screaming in agony and Apollo on the floor fast asleep,

Chapter 8

The baby was fine and the nurses checked on Apollo he was alright he just fainted, when the new family got home there was a white envelope in the letter box it had red and gold silk woven into it.

he opened the letter and read it, " Dear Mr Stone I am writing to you today to formaly invited you to Buckingham Palace to talk about you becoming the new priminister you are verry brave and inspiring and your Father in-law was going to be the priminister too. P.S congratulations on the baby when you come please tell me the name.

yours scincerely The Queen xx
"

" OMG! well done honey can't believe it i am so proud of you " replied Melinda full of excitement

" Well well well so you took my job " spoke David as super speeded in the room

Melinda walked up to her Father and snapped his neck, as Melinda looked at her Father she said " How dare you ever come to this house you evil monster "

THE NEXT DAY

Today was the day the family were going to Buckingham Palace they got in the car, and set off it took them 4 hours to get to london, the Guards opened the huge, 9-golden, royal gates and stepped in, the doors opened and they were led to the Queen. They were sitting down at the table sipping tea and eating crumpets as they talked for hours and then the Queen said " so are you gonna tell me the cute babies name " " oh yeah it's Stephan " replied Apollo suddenly the ground started to skake and the antiques and pictures were flying off the shelves then the big, Gold stone door opened and one of the

Queens messengers
stepped in and shouted
in a panic vioce " my
Queen there is bombers
and terrorists attacking
the Palace, some of them
are already in "

" how did they get past
the guards " the Queen
replied

" because the guards are
dead, they bombed all

the guards at the gates "
is how the the
messenger answered her
question.

Chapter 9

Then suddenly the the
doors swung open, and
the terrorists pionted
the guns at there heads
and threatend to kill
them if they did not do
what they said. The four

of them (Melinda, Apollo, The Queen and the Queens Messenger) lay there face down tho the ground when the Queen remebered she always carried a spare pistol gun, so she said to the guards " men look behind you " giving her enough time to slip the gun out and shoot one of the terrorists the men

gathered around the
wounded man and then
Melinda grabbed
Stephan and they all ran
off and one of the
terrorists stabbed the
Queen and she dropped
Apollo grabbed her and
speeded them to the
helicopter on the roof,
then the men ran out,
and started to shoot the
big, blue helicopter when

they were soon stopped
becuse they were shot
by the police, the Queen
was slowly dieng in the
helicopter and then they
finaly landed on the car
park of a hospital and
the doctors quickly
rushed in. It was not long
before the doctor came
back out and announced
to Melinda and Apollo
and the messenger that

the Queen passed away
because she bled to
death it was finaly the
day that Apollo was
becoming Prime Minister
and he was so happy he
got the keys to the door
number 10 downing
street and they lived a
good life Stephan went
to an incredible school
Apollo work as the Prime
Minister and Melinda was

a waitress at pizza hut and a part time job at Gregg's everything was perfect and the best bit of all was that Marco is finaly gone OR WAS HE......

Chapter 10

Somewhere amongst the rocky hills of Translyvania Lay Marco, who was planning his evil revenge against Apollo, Stephen, and Melinda but this time it was no bite it was troule and by this I meant that alot of people were going to die and in not a nice way, he's coming guys and his staying for good but are you? that is the ultimate question but for now Apolo was settling in in Number Ten downing

street whilst Melinda
was working double
shifts in her local Pizza
hut and Gregg's Bakery,

<u>Message From The Teen</u>
<u>Authors</u>

Thankyou for reading this
short teaser novel by me
Joshua Mark Foster and

Jack Trevor Foster this was a short novel just to kick start both of our writing careers and get a novel out there for viewers to read and see if they like our writing and our ways of storytelling

Thanks

Joshua Foster,

Jack Foster.

2017